BE PART OF THE TEAM!

ON THE
HOCKEY
TEAM

STEPHANE HILLARD

PowerKiDS press

New York

Published in 2022 by The Rosen Publishing Group, Inc.
29 East 21st Street, New York, NY 10010

First Edition

Portions of this work were originally authored by Greg Roza and published as *Hockey*. All new material in this edition was authored by Stephane Hillard.

Editor: Greg Roza
Book Design: Michael Flynn

Photo Credits: Cover (hockey players) Thomas Barwick/Stone/Getty Images; cover, pp. 8, 10, 20 (hockey puck) pikepicture/iStock/Getty Images; p. 4 Kevin Brine/iStock/Getty Images; p. 5 LuckyBusiness/iStock/Getty Images; p. 7 Stephanie Bianchetti/Corbis Historical/Getty Images; pp. 9, 11 Dmytro Aksonov/E+/Getty Images; p. 13 master1305/iStock/Getty Images; p. 15 Fotosearch/Getty Images; p. 16 George Silk/The LIFE Picture Collection/Getty Images; p. 17 PM Images/Stone/Getty Images; p. 19 Score/Aflo/Getty Images; p. 21 Harry How/Getty Images.

Library of Congress Cataloging-in-Publication Data

Names: Hillard, Stephane, author.
Title: On the hockey team / Stephane Hillard.
Description: New York : PowerKids Press, [2022] | Series: Be part of the team! | Includes index.
Identifiers: LCCN 2020037568 | ISBN 9781725327719 (library binding) | ISBN 9781725327696 (paperback) | ISBN 9781725327702 (6 pack)
Subjects: LCSH: Hockey–Juvenile literature. | Teamwork (Sports)–Juvenile literature.
Classification: LCC GV847.25 .H55 2022 | DDC 796.962–dc23
LC record available at https://lccn.loc.gov/2020037568

Manufactured in the United States of America

Some of the images in this book illustrate individuals who are models. The depictions do not imply actual situations or events.

CPSIA Compliance Information: Batch #CSPK22. For Further Information contact Rosen Publishing, New York, New York at 1-800-237-9932.

Find us on

CONTENTS

TEAM PLAYERS. 4

THE HISTORY OF HOCKEY. 6

ON THE RINK. 8

GAME TIME. 10

GOAL! 12

PLAYERS ON DEFENSE 14

THE GOALIE 16

PLAYING BY THE RULES 18

PRO HOCKEY. 20

GLOSSARY 22

FOR MORE INFORMATION 23

INDEX 24

TEAM PLAYERS

There are several different kinds of hockey. This book is about ice hockey, which is played on an ice surface called a rink. Hockey players wear ice skates. Teammates use special sticks to pass a puck around the rink until they can shoot it into the goal for a point.

A hockey team may have 20 players, but only six players are on the ice at one time. The action is fast, and players on the ice get tired quickly. Teamwork is important!

HOCKEY PUCK

Hockey players wear a lot of **equipment** to keep themselves safe. This includes a helmet, face guard, gloves, and many pads.

THE HISTORY OF HOCKEY

Ice hockey most likely began in Canada. In the early 1800s, British soldiers in Canada played several ball-and-stick games, including a game similar to field hockey. Some began playing the game on ponds covered with ice. By the late 1800s, ice hockey had become a popular sport in Canada and the United States.

Today, hockey is an Olympic sport, and **professional** hockey is played in countries around the world. People still like to play ice hockey outside. It's sometimes called "pond hockey."

TEAM TALK

In March 1875, the first indoor hockey game happened in Montreal, Quebec. The rink was much smaller than local ponds. The teams were limited to 9 players each.

In this painting from 1898, a group of fashionable women play hockey on the lake in Wimbledon Park in London, England.

ON THE RINK

Ice rinks have a goal at each end with some space behind each goal. Two blue lines split a rink into three different **zones**. The area closest to a team's own goal is the **defending** zone. The zone in the middle is the **neutral** zone. The area farthest from a team's goal is the attacking zone.

Each game starts with a face-off. This happens in the circle at center ice. Face-offs can happen in any of the circles after play stops for a **penalty**.

GOAL

FACE-OFF CIRCLE

BLUE LINE

BLUE LINE

RED LINE

GOAL

TEAM TALK

During a face-off, one player from each team faces the other while an **official** drops the puck on the ice between them.

A face-off at center ice also occurs after a goal is scored.

GAME TIME

A hockey game is 60 minutes long, with three 20-minute periods. The clock stops after goals, when a penalty occurs, and when someone gets hurt.

To score, players on a team use their sticks to shoot the puck into the other team's goal. That's called offense. Players also try to keep the other team from shooting the puck into their goal. That's called defense. Teams change back and forth between offense and defense very quickly. Hockey is a fast-paced game!

The goalie is the player who stands right in front of the goal. They make exciting saves and help their team set up plays.

11

GOAL!

When teammates are on offense, they skate toward the other team's goal. They must have good stick-handling skills to keep the other team from stealing the puck from them. They must be good skaters to get around the other team.

Players on offense pass the puck back and forth, looking for a chance to shoot. They can take slap shots by raising their sticks and shooting the puck hard. They can take wrist shots by shooting the puck quickly off the tip of their sticks.

TEAM TALK

Each team has three forwards on the ice at one time. Forwards are great scorers! The player in the middle is called the center. The players on either side of the center are called wingers.

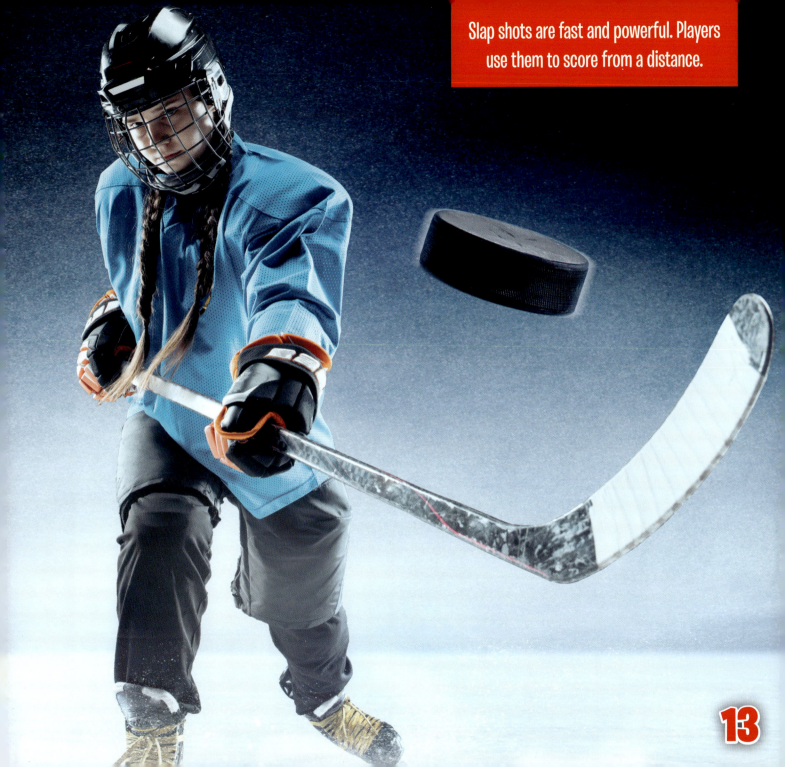

Slap shots are fast and powerful. Players use them to score from a distance.

PLAYERS ON DEFENSE

When teammates are on defense, they must stop the other team from reaching their goal and scoring points. They can do this by **intercepting** a pass. They can use their strength and speed to check, or bump, an offensive player away from the puck. They can also use their stick or body to block a shot on goal.

Defensive players must be strong to keep the offense from skating by them. They must be quick enough to grab the puck with their sticks when they have a chance.

TEAM TALK

Each team has two defenders on the ice at one time. They play closer to their own goalie and stop the other team from scoring. Defenders help out on offense too.

Checking is used to bump a player and take the puck from them. It's an important defensive play during a game of hockey.

15

THE GOALIE

The goalie stands in front of their team's goal and stops the puck from going into it. This player is the last line of defense for the team.

Goalie pads are bigger to keep them safe from flying pucks and crashing players. They wear helmets with facemasks. Goalies use a basket-like glove to catch hard shots. The other glove has a wide pad on the back for blocking shots. A goalie stick is larger than regular sticks for the same reason.

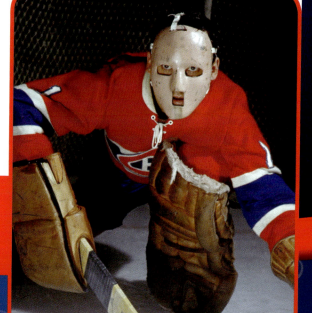

Long ago, hockey players didn't wear facemasks! In 1959, Canadian Jacques Plante (shown here) became the first goalie to regularly wear a mask.

PLAYING BY THE RULES

Hockey has many rules! For example, players can't pass the puck with their hands. Some rules help keep players safe. Players can't check another player from behind. They can't use their stick to trip other players.

When a player breaks a rule, an official calls a penalty. The player must sit in an area called the penalty box for at least 2 minutes. Their team must play with one less player during that time! This makes it easier for the other team to score.

TEAM TALK

Major penalties—such as fighting—result in 4 minutes or more in the penalty box. A player might also be removed from the game for major penalties.

Two-minute penalties—such as hooking and slashing with the stick—are called minor penalties.

19

PRO HOCKEY

No hockey player can win a game alone. It takes teamwork! Players on offense need to help out their teammates on defense. Defensive players help get the offensive players in place to score a goal. All the players need to support the goalie.

Hockey players who work hard enough often go on to higher levels. Some make it onto professional teams in the National Hockey League (NHL)! Even the superstars of hockey need teammates to be successful.

HOCKEY TALK

ASSIST	A PASS TO A TEAMMATE, WHO THEN SCORES.
BACK-CHECK	TO RUSH TO THE DEFENDING ZONE IN RESPONSE TO A QUICK ATTACK FROM THE OTHER TEAM.
BREAKAWAY	WHEN A PLAYER HAS THE PUCK AND THERE ARE NO OTHER PLAYERS BETWEEN THAT PLAYER AND THE OTHER TEAM'S GOALIE.
FORECHECK	TO CHECK PLAYERS ON THE OTHER TEAM IN AN ATTEMPT TO SET UP A SCORING PLAY IN THE ATTACKING ZONE.
HAT TRICK	WHEN ONE PLAYER SCORES THREE GOALS IN ONE GAME.
POWER PLAY	THE TIME WHILE ONE TEAM HAS MORE PLAYERS ON THE ICE THAN THE OTHER TEAM, DUE TO PENALTIES.
ODD-MAN RUSH	WHEN MORE OFFENSIVE PLAYERS ENTER THE ATTACKING ZONE THAN THERE ARE DEFENSIVE PLAYERS THERE.
SHORTHANDED	MISSING PLAYERS DUE TO PENALTIES.

GLOSSARY

defending: Having to do with stopping the other team from scoring.

equipment: The supplies and tools needed to do something.

intercept: To take a pass meant for a player on the other team.

neutral: Not favoring either side in a contest.

official: A person who makes sure that players are following the rules of a game.

penalty: A loss one team or player must take for breaking a rule.

professional: Having to do with an activity that someone gets paid to do.

zone: An area that is different from surrounding areas in some way.

FOR MORE INFORMATION

BOOKS

Scheff, Max. *The Stanley Cup Finals: Hockey's Greatest Tournament.* Minneapolis, MN: Lerner Publications, 2020.

Sherman, Jill. *Hockey.* Hopkins, MN: Bellwether Media, 2019.

WEBSITES

Hockey Fact for Kids
kids.kiddle.co/Hockey
Read fascinating facts about different types of hockey, including ice and field hockey.

Basic Ice Hockey Rules
www.kids-sports-activities.com/ice-hockey-rules.html
Learn more about the rules of hockey.

INDEX

C
center, 12
check, 14, 15, 18, 21

D
defender, 14
defense, 10, 14, 16, 20

F
forward, 12

G
goalie, 11, 14, 16, 20, 21

N
National Hockey Association (NHL), 20

O
offense, 10, 12, 14, 20
official, 9, 18

P
penalties, 8, 10, 18, 19, 21
Plante, Jacques, 16

R
rules, 18

W
winger, 12

Z
zones, 8, 21